LANGUAGES OF INDIA FOR KIDS

DHRUV GAMI

ILLUSTRATED BY SONA & JACOB

Dedication

This book is dedicated to
all the curious and courageous kids,
including my inspirations Anvesha and Abhiti.

A huge thanks to my wife, Dhvani,
for her enthusiastic support of this project,
and to Sona and Jacob
for their expert guidance and creative excellence.

This book belongs to

....

....

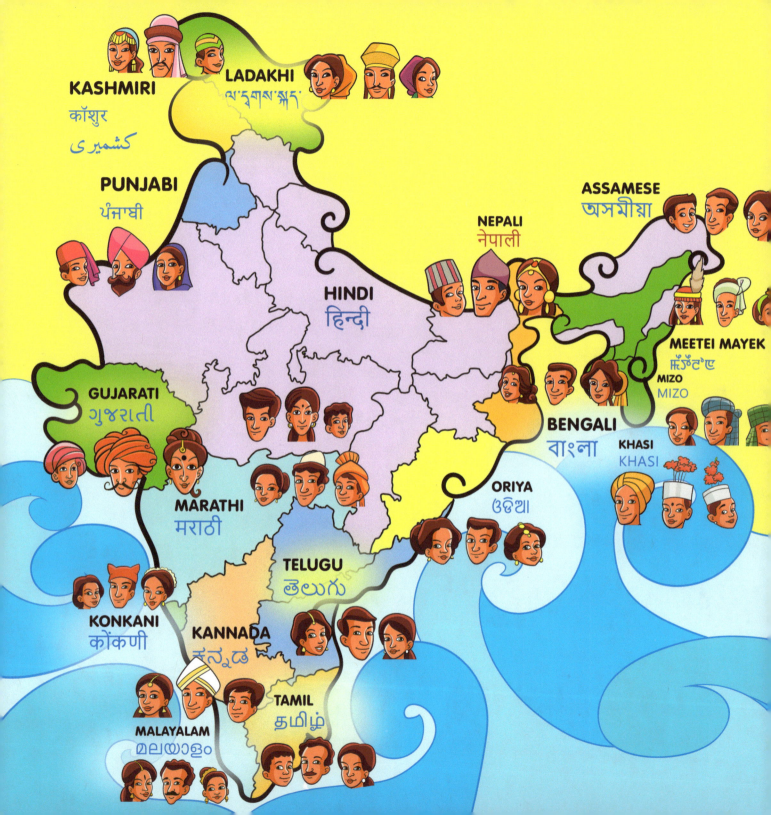

INDIA IS A BIG COUNTRY. PEOPLE SPEAK DIFFERENT LANGUAGES ACROSS THE COUNTRY.

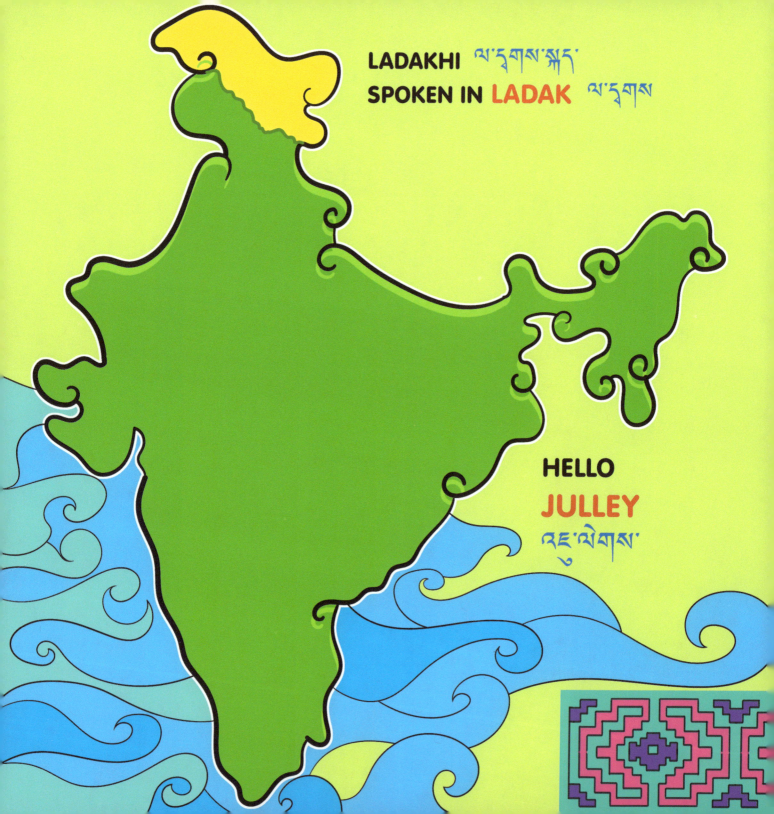

THANK YOU
JULLEY
འཇུ་ལེགས་

GOODBYE
JULLEY
འཇུ་ལེགས་

HOW ARE YOU?
(SKU) KHAMZANG IN-A LEY
(སྐུ་)ཁམས་བཟང་ཡིན་ན་ལེགས།

I AM FINE
KHAMZANG IN LEY
ཁམས་བཟང་ཡིན་ལེགས།

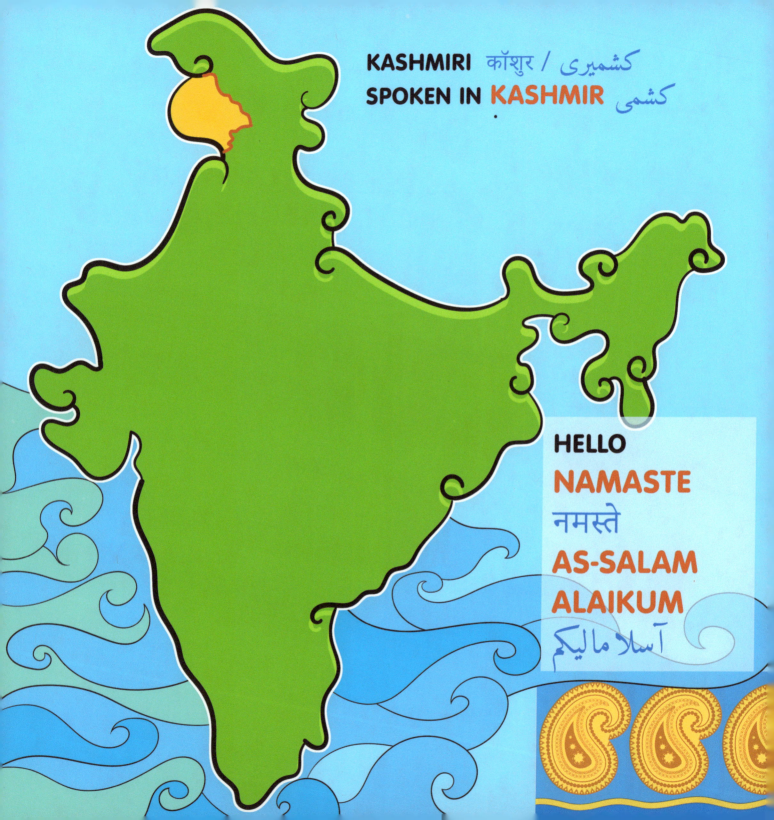

THANK YOU
SHUKRIYA
शुक्रिया / شکریہ

GOODBYE
NAMASTE
नमस्ते
KHUDA HAFAZ
خدا حافظ

HOW ARE YOU?
TOHAY CHHIVA VAARAY?
तोहय छिवा वारय्?
تہي چھِہِ حض وارِ پأٹھ؟

I AM FINE
AHN HAZ VAARAY
आंन् हज़ वारय्
اہَن حض وارے

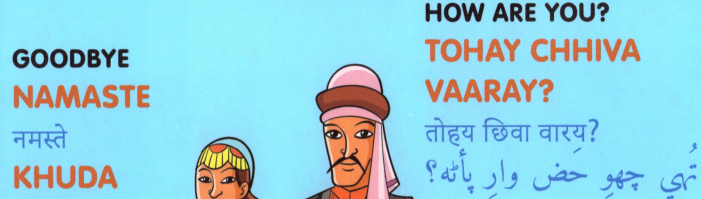

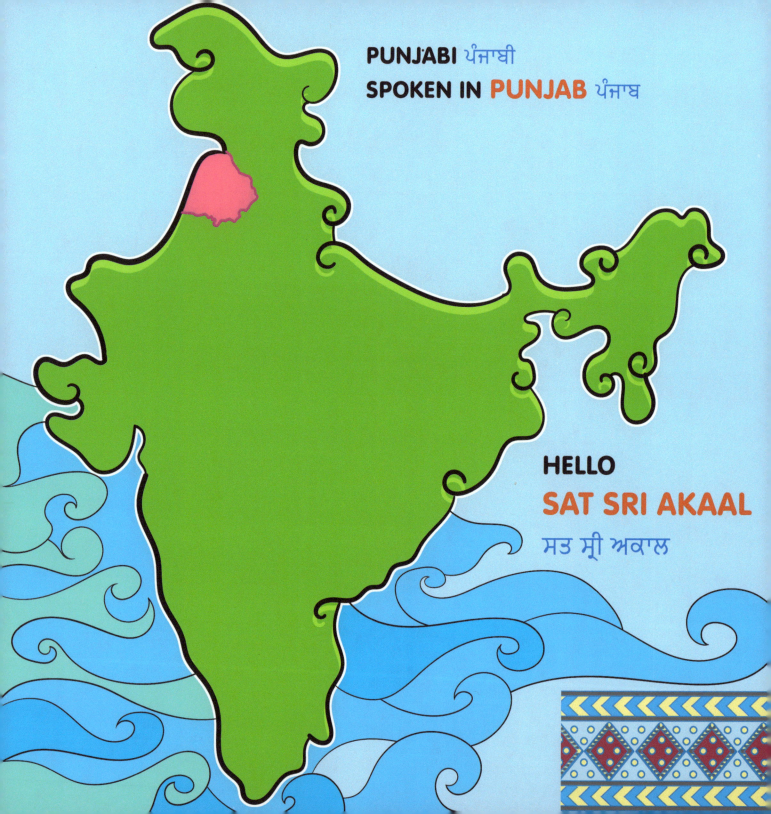

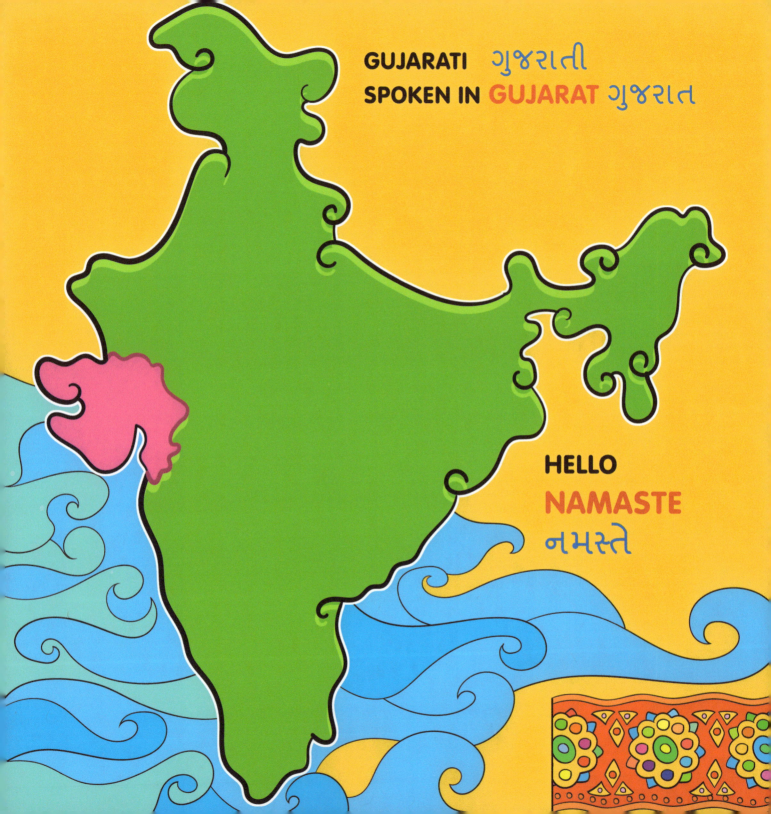

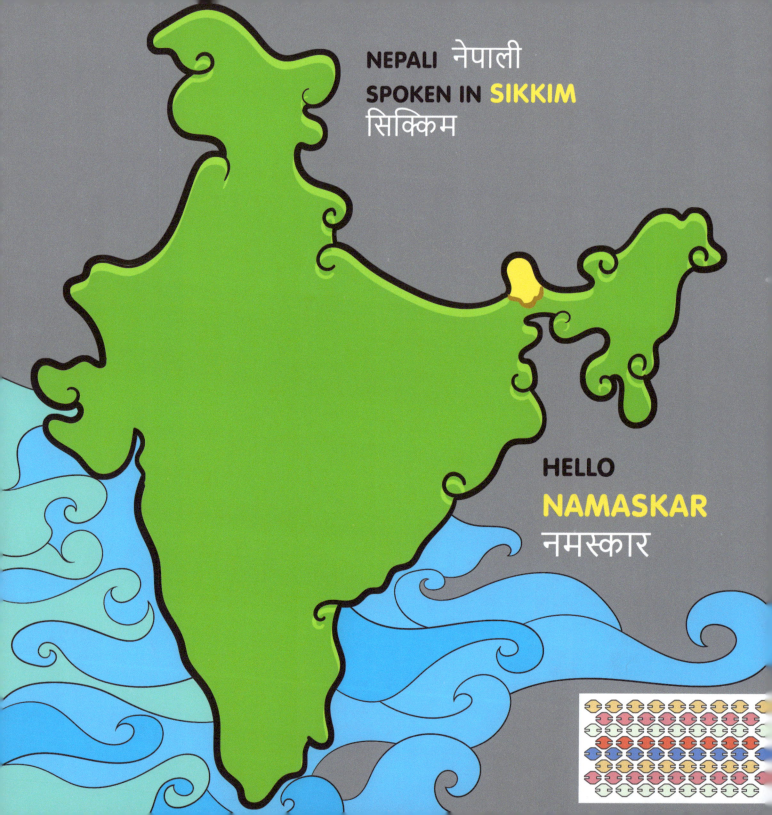

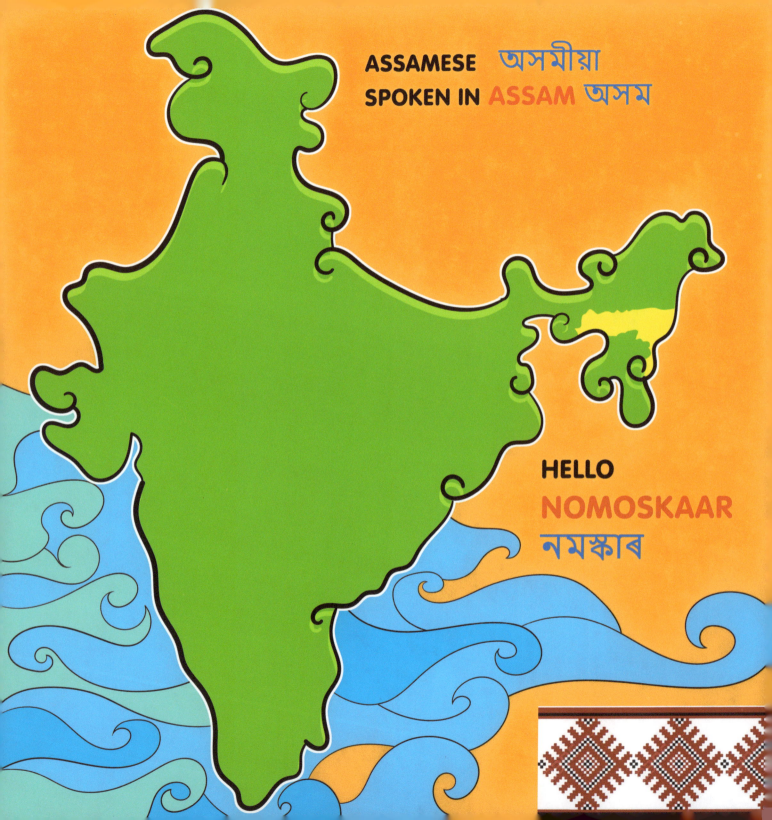

THANK YOU
DHONYOBAAD
ধন্যবাদ

GOODBYE
BIDAAYE
বিদায়

HOW ARE YOU?
AAPUNI KENE ASSE?
আপুনি কেনে আছে?

I AM FINE
BHAALE ASSU
ভালে আছোঁ

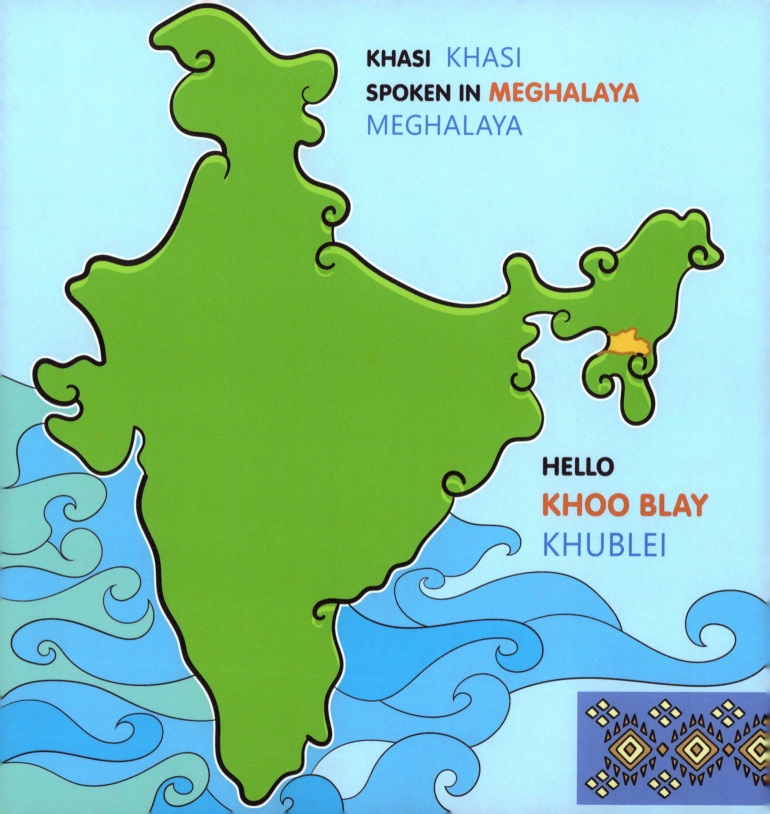

THANK YOU
KHOO BLAY
KHUBLEI

GOODBYE
KHOO BLAY
KHUBLEI

HOW ARE YOU?
KOOM NO?
KUMNO?

I AM FINE
KOOM NAY
KUMNE

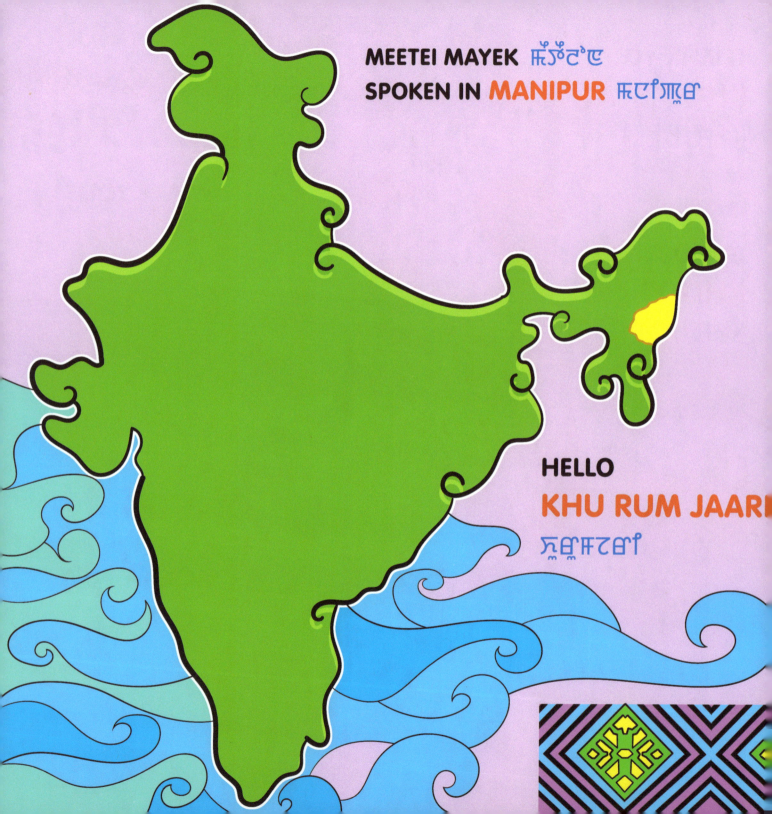

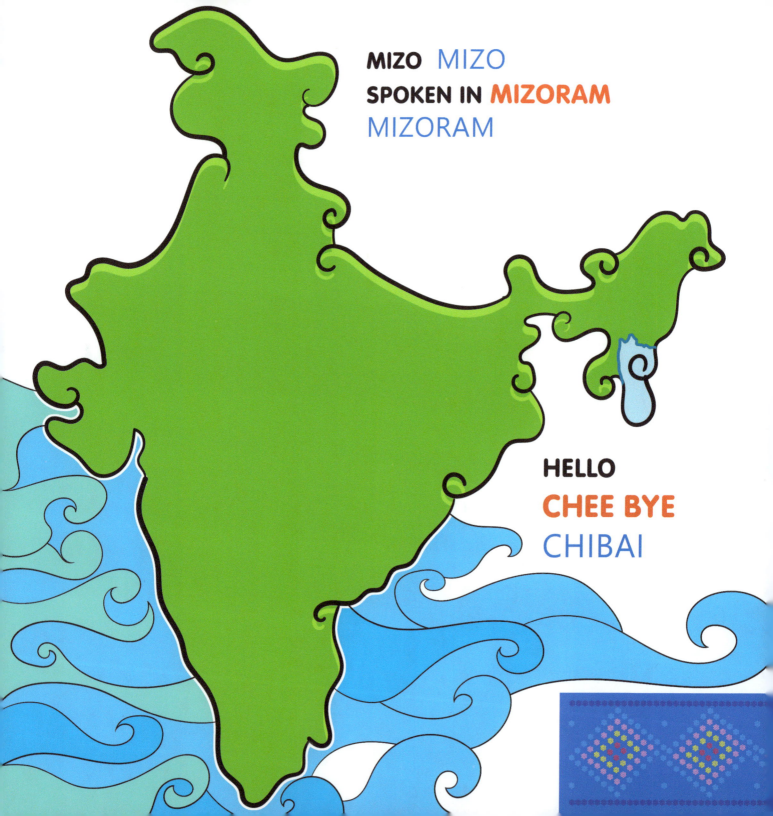

THANK YOU
KA LOM A
KA LAWM E

GOODBYE
MANGTHRA
MANGHA

HOW ARE YOU?
AY DAM MO
I DAM MAW?

I AM FINE
KA DAM A
KA DAM E

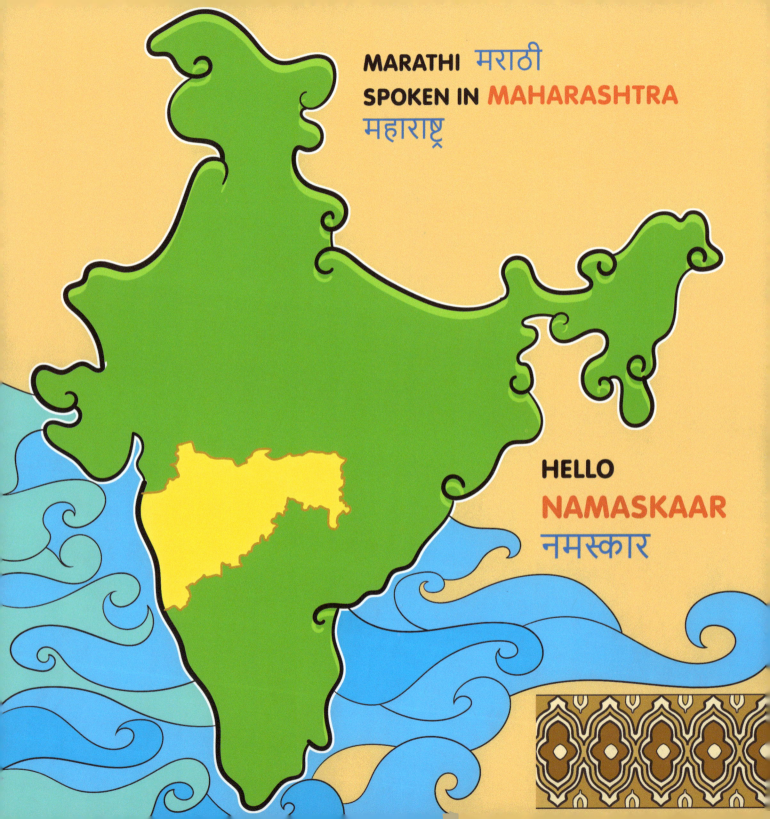

THANK YOU
DHANYAVAAD
धन्यवाद

GOODBYE
NIROP
निरोप

HOW ARE YOU?
TU KASA AAHES
तू कसा आहेस?

I AM FINE
MEE THEEK AAHE
मी ठीक आहे

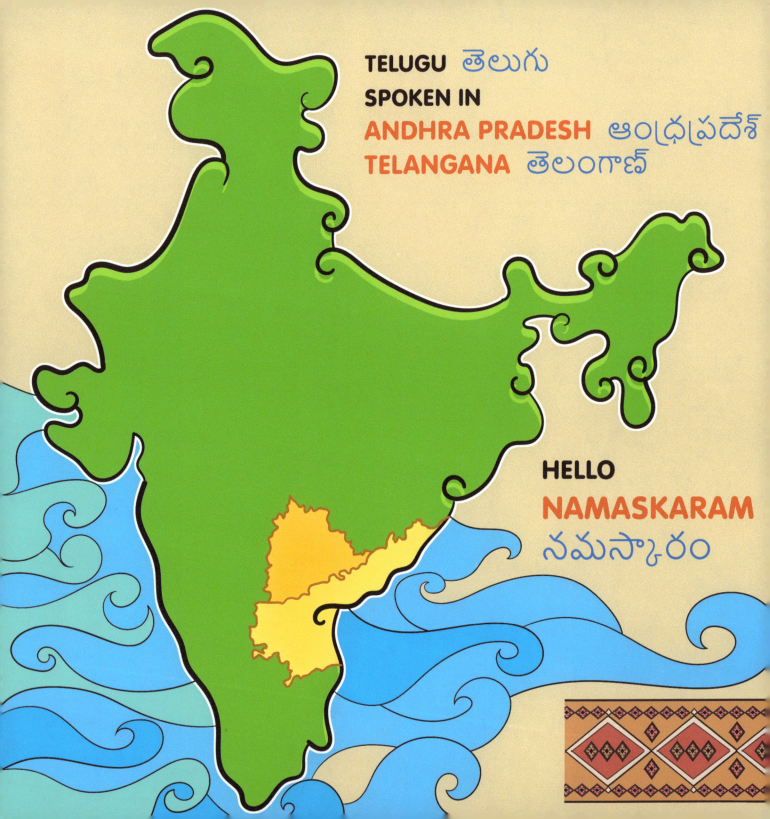

THANK YOU
DHANYAVAAD-ALU
ధన్యవాదాలు

GOODBYE
VEEDKOLU
వీడ్కోలు

HOW ARE YOU?
MIRU ELAA UNNARU
మీరు ఎలా ఉన్నారు?

I AM FINE
NENU BAGUN-NANU
నేను బాగున్నాను

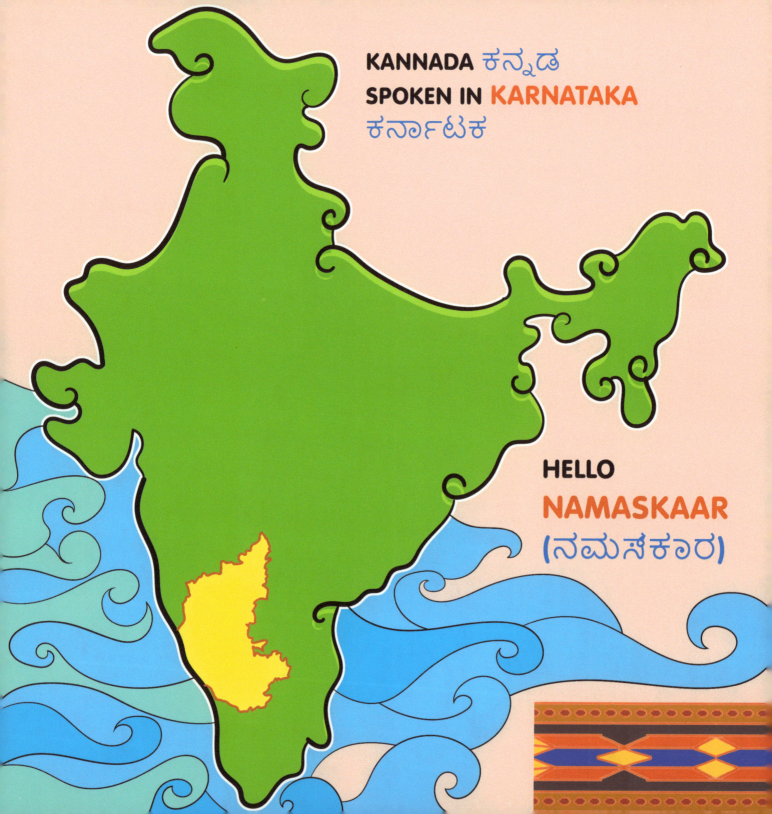

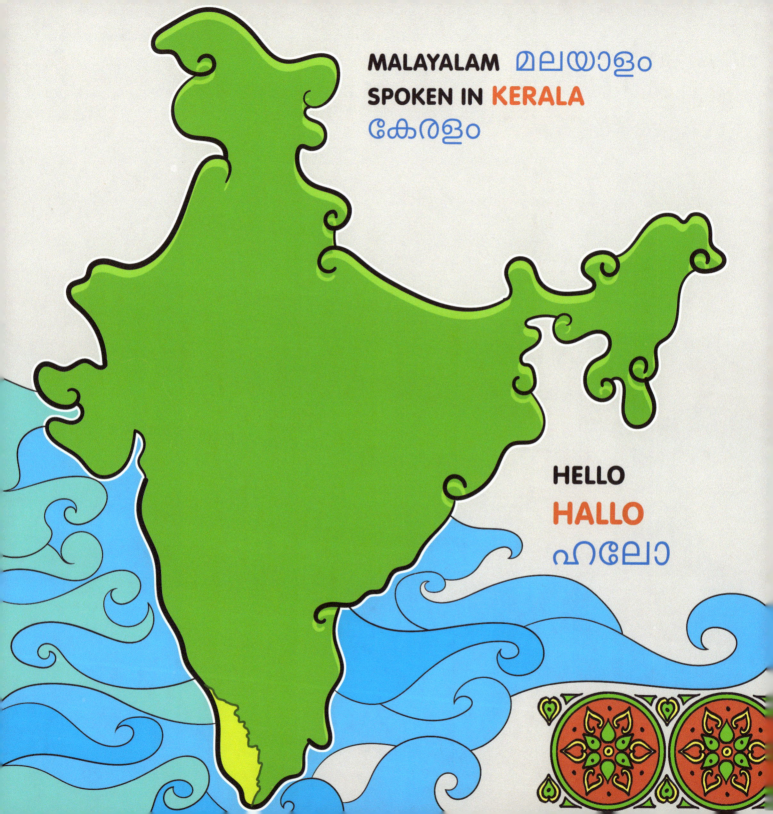

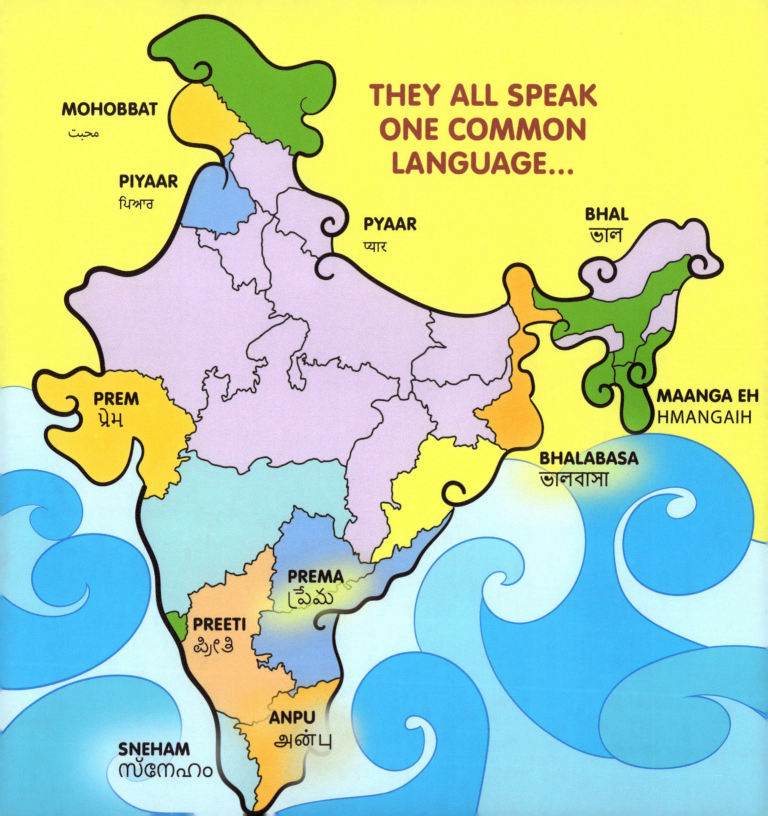

CPSIA information can be obtained
at www.ICGtesting.com
Printed in the USA
BVHW062022201022
649777BV00002B/11